ISBN 978-1-333-75916-2
PIBN 10544342

1 MONTH OF
FREE
READING

at

www.ForgottenBooks.com

By purchasing this book you are eligible for one month membership to ForgottenBooks.com, giving you unlimited access to our entire collection of over 700,000 titles via our web site and mobile apps.

To claim your free month visit:

www.forgottenbooks.com/free544342

English
Français
Deutsche
Italiano
Español
Português

www.forgottenbooks.com

Mythology Photography **Fiction**
Fishing Christianity **Art** Cooking
Essays Buddhism Freemasonry
Medicine **Biology** Music **Ancient
Egypt** Evolution Carpentry Physics
Dance Geology **Mathematics** Fitness
Shakespeare **Folklore** Yoga Marketing
Confidence Immortality Biographies
Poetry **Psychology** Witchcraft
Electronics Chemistry History **Law**
Accounting **Philosophy** Anthropology
Alchemy Drama Quantum Mechanics
Atheism Sexual Health **Ancient History**
Entrepreneurship Languages Sport
Paleontology Needlework Islam
Metaphysics Investment Archaeology
Parenting Statistics Criminology
Motivational

This book must not
be taken from the
Library building.

Procceedings of Stock-
holders of

North Carolina
Railroad
Company

Fifty-Sixth Annual Meeting

Greensboro, N. C.
July 12th, 1906

North Carolina Railroad Co.

..PROCEEDINGS OF..
THL STOCKHOLDERS

Fifth-Sixth Annual Meeting

Greensboro, N. C., July 12th, 1906

PROCEEDINGS

OF THE FIFTY SIXTH ANNUAL
MEETING OF THE

STOCKHOLDERS
NORTH CAROLINA RAILROAD
COMPANY

STOCKHOLDERS MEETING

Greensboro, N. C., July 12, 1906.

The stockholders of the North Carolina Railroad Company, in pursuance of notice duly given, met in the City of Greensboro. at the Benbow Hotel, on July 12, 1906, at 2:30 o'clock P. M.

Upon motion of Mr. H. G. Chatham, Col. B. Cameron was called to the chair, and Mr. A. H. Eller was appointed to act as Secretary of the meeting.

The President called for a reading of the minutes of the last preceding meeting, which were approved.

Mr. C. D. Benbow, on behalf of the Proxy Committee, reported that there were 170 stockholders present, and that they represented 7653 shares of stock, 1407 being represented in person and 6246 being represented by proxy. The Chairman announced that under the by-laws of the Company there were a sufficient number of stockholders and sufficient amount of stock represented for the transaction of business, and declared the meeting duly organized and ready for business.

President H. G. Chatham then submitted his report, together with the report of the Finance Committee, and the Secretary and Treasurer and the Expert, the same having been printed It was ordered that reading of the said reports be dispensed with, and the Secretary and Treasurer was ordered to have the same, together with the proceedings of this meeting, published in pamphlet form.

Mr. P. C. Pope, the State's proxy, was present and presented his commission or credentials and cast the vote of the stock owned by the State for the following persons as directors for the ensuing year, to-wit : H. G. Chatham, W. H. Williams, W. T. Brown, Thos. H. Vanderford, John W. Lambeth, Allen J. Ruffin, S. C. Penn and L. Banks Holt, and the said persons were declared unanimously elected.

Mr. W. H. Williams then nominated as directors on the part of private stockholders the following persons : Gen. R. T. Hoke, Col. B. Cameron, Col. W. E. Holt and Mr. Hugh McRae. Upon motion, the Secretary was ordered to cast the vote of the stockholders for the said persons as directors. The Secretary reported that he had cast the vote of all stock represented, to-wit: Thirty-seven thousand six hundred and fifty-three votes, and the said persons were declared duly elected directors for the ensuing year.

Upon motion, the Secretary was ordered to cast the vote for all stockholders present for the following persons as members of the Finance Committee, to-wit· W. T. Hollowell, J. G. Steed, R. R. Ray, C. O. McMichael and A. C. Avery, Jr., on the part of the State, and Col. B. Cameron and Col. W. E. Holt on the part of the private stockholders. The Secretary announced that he had so cast the vote of all stock present, and the said persons were declared elected.

Mr. P. C. Pope, the State's proxy, nominated Mr. C. D. Benbow and Mr. L. M. Michaux as members of the Proxy Committee for the ensuing year, and said persons were duly elected.

Gen. R. F. Hoke then offered the following, as an amendment to the by-laws, to-wit: Under the head of "Meeting of the Stockholders," Section V, strike out the word "two," in line four, and insert in lieu thereof the word "one," and add to said section the following: "And one newspaper published in the city of Greensboro or Charlotte, and notice shall be given at the same time, that the transfer books will be closed for ten days prior to said meeting." And under the head of "Transfers," Section I, strike out the two last lines of Paragraph I, and insert in lieu thereof "10 days prior to the dividend periods in February and August," of which notice shall be given for ten days prior to said closing in two newspapers—one published in the City of Raleigh and one in Greensboro or Charlotte."—Adopted.

It was further moved and carried as follows:

That the Secretary and Treasurer be requested to prepare a general revisal of the by-laws of the Company and submit the same to the next meeting of the stockholders.

There being no further business, the meeting adjourned.

B. CAMERON, Chairman.

A. H. ALLER, Secretary.

PRESIDENT'S REPORT.

North Carolina Railroad Co.

President's Office.

Burlington, N. C., July, 3, 1906.

To the Stockholders and Board of Directors of the North Carolina Railroad Company.

Gentlemen: In accordance with the By-laws of your Company I submit the reports of your Secretary and Treasurer, Expert and Finance Committee. You will be gratified to note the continued strengthening of your financial position and the consequent increased value of your property. Fortified by your wise policy of conservatism and economy the further appreciation of the stock of your Company is not only probable but assured.   Respectfully submitted,

H. G. Chatham,
President.

REPORT OF FINANCE COMMITTE E.

Burlington, N. C., June 28th, 1906.

To the Stockholders of the North Carolina Railroad Co.

Your Finance Committee reports as follows: We have this day examined the books and accounts of the Treasurer, and found them correct, and properly and neatly kept. We have further examined the dividend and stock books and find them likewise correct and in order. The amount of cash balance on hand June 1st, 1906, as shown by the books, was $11,881.15 This we have verified by reference to amounts deposited in bank, and by counting cash on hand in vault.

The sum of $1,012 16 has been received from S. A. L. Ry., since last annual report, to cover this road's portion of back taxes on Union Depot at Raleigh, N. C. This covering taxes up to and including the year 1904.

We find that from June 1st, 1905, to June 1st, 1906, the sum of $2,700 has been received from the sale of Real Estate. Respectfully submitted.

A. C. AVERY, Jr.
J. G. STEED
W. T. HOLLOWELL
CHAS O. MCMICHAEL.
Finance Committee.

Secretary and Treasurer's Report.

BURLINGTON, N. C., JULY 12, 1906.

To the Stockholders of the North Carolina Railroad Co.:

GENTLEMEN:—I herewith submit the annual statement of the North Carolina Railroad Company, showing the financial condition for the fiscal year ending May 31, 1906, also statement of receipts and disbursements of the Company for the same period.

Very Respectfully,
A. H. ELLER,
Sec'y & Treas.

Financial Condition of the North Carolina Railroad Company

ASSETS

PROPERTY ASSETS			
Construction and Equipment_____	$ 4,975,627 53		
State University Railroad Stock__	5,000 00	$ 4,980,627 53	
CASH ASSETS			
Dividend Tax_____	17 95		
Bills Receivable_____	300 00	317 95	
Cash on hand May 31, 1906_____	11,881 15	11.881 15	
		$ 4,992,826 63	

for Fiscal Year Ending May 31, 1906.

LAIBILITIES

Capital Stock_____		$ 4,000,000	00
Profit and Loss_____		849,708	13
FLOATING DEBT			
Dividend Certificates_____	108 00		
Unpaid Dividends_____	2,961 50		
3½ per cent on dividend No. 44 due August 1, 1906 _____	140,049 00		
		143,118	50
		$ 4,992,826	63

Receipts and Disbursements of the Treasurer N. C. R. R. Co.

RECEIPTS

From Lease of Road	$ 286,000	00	
Lease of Union Passenger Station Raleigh, N. C.	988	80	
From Sale of Real Estate	2,700	00	
Dividend Checks Withdrawn	67	00	
Taxes from S. A. L.	1,119	74	$ 290,875 54
Cash on hand June 1, 1905			7,590 46
			$ 298,466 00

from June 1st, 1905 to June 1st, 1906

DISBURSEMENTS

Dividends Paid	$ 280,090 50		
Salaries and Fees	4,306 86		
Incidentals	2,187 49	$ 286,584 85	
Cash on hand June 1, 1906		11,881 15	
		$ 298,466 00	

REPORT OF LAND COMMITTEE.

July 11, 1906.

Mr. H. G. Chatham, President North Carolina Railroad Company:

DEAR SIR : The Land Committee report that for the year ending May 31, 1906, the sum of $2,700.00 has been paid into the Treasury for lots sold at Burlington, N. C.

They also report that they sold today one lot for $200.00 cash.

Yours respectfully,

R. F. HOKE,

L. BANKS HOLT,

A. J. RUFFIN,

Land Committee.

EXPERT'S REPORT.

Greensboro, N. C., Dec. 27, 1905.

Mr. Samuel Spencer, President, Southern Railway Co., No. 80 Broadway, New York City, and Mr. H. G. Chatham, President, North Carolina Railroad, Elkin, N. C.

GENTLEMEN: We have to report that the North Carolina Railroad was examined by us from Goldsboro, N. C., to Charlotte, N. C

From Goldsboro to Selma, N. C., the road has not been ballasted as recommended in previous report, but we find that all of the 50 pound rail, with the exception of about 2 1-4 miles, has been replaced with 60 pound rails and that cross ties have been put in track which brings this part of the line up to a better standard than last year.

From Selma, N. C., to Greensboro, N. C., we find that the road has been maintained in good condition; that approximately 17 1-2 miles of 75 pound rail has been laid, replacing 60 pound rail. A large number of new ties have been put in track and the road has been maintained in good condition, showing an improvement over last year.

The hotel at Burlington that was burned (mention of which was made in last report) has not yet been replaced.

From Greensboro to Charlotte, N. C., we find the road to be in first-class condition, showing an improvement over last year in ballast and timbering.

We find the entire road-bed from Goldsboro, N. C., to Charlotte, N. C., has been maintained, ditches have been kept in general good condition and embankments have in many places been strengthened; cross ties are good and renewals have been kept up to the necessary standard between the above terminals.

The following list shows the more important betterments that have been made since last examination.

BETWEEN GOLDSBORO AND GREENSBORO

RAIL

185,856 feet of 75 pound relay steel rail laid, releasing 60 pound rail between Greensboro and Selma.

76,454 feet of 60 pound relay steel rail laid between Selma and Goldsboro, releasing 50 pound relay steel.

BALLAST

13,583 cubic yards of crushed stone ballast put in between Greensboro and Selma.

Side Tracks Constructed

LOCATION	FOR WHAT PURPOSE	FEET
Graham	Midway Brick Co	350
Goldsboro	Dewey Bros	328
Gibsonville	Minneola Manufacturing Co	350
Selma	N. E. Ward	600
Selma	Navassa Guano Co	3250
Haw River	Trollingwood Manufacturing Co	27-25
Hillsboro	Bellevue Manufacturing Co	1000
Selma	Storage Tracks	11500
Durham	Bad order car track	250
Durham	Re-arrangement tracks, account Union Station, no new track	
Durham	AmericanTobacco Co	1140
Goldsboro	H. Weil & Bro	275
		21768

Cross Ties

Number used in renewals, main track	56,135
Number used in renewals, side tracks	3,959
Number used in new side tracks	6,333
	66,427

Switch Ties

Number sets used in renewals	22
Number sets used in new side tracks	23
	45

Bridges

Little River: Second hand bridge span erected, releasing lighter span.

Trestles

No extensive work done.

Buildings

None.

Undergrade Crossings

None.

Water Stations, Coaling Stations, Culverts

None.

BETWEEN GREENSBORO AND SPENCER

RAIL

None laid.

BALLAST

39,290 cubic yards crushed stone ballast put in between Greensboro and Spencer.

Side Tracks Constructed

LOCATION	FOR WHAT PURPOSE	FEET
High Point	Tomlinson Chair Co	400
Greensboro	Wysong & Miles	145
Greensboro	Merchants Grocery Co	365
Greensboro	Guilford Plaster Co	522
Thomasville	Thomasville Chair Co	700
Jamestown	Passing track	3100
High Point	Yard changes	10470
High Point	High Point Pipe and Foundry Co	1000
		16702

Cross Ties

Number used in renewals, main track ----- 19,284
Number used in renewals, side tracks ----- 3,704
Number used in new side tracks ----- 11,771

34,759

Switch Ties

Number of sets used in renewals ----- 7
Number of sets used in new side tracks ----- 27

34

Bridges

No extension work done.

Trestles

No extension work done.

Buildings

LOCATION	NATURE OF WORK DONE
Lexington	New section foreman's house.
High Point	Transfer platform.
Pomona	New signal tour and interlocking plant.

Undergrade Crossings

Lexington : New subway put in, releasing grade crossing.

Water Stations

Yadkin River to Spencer, eight inch pipe line laid.

Coaling Stations

None.

Culverts

None.

BETWEEN SPENCER AND CHARLOTTE

RAIL

No new rail laid except a few feet for switch leads in connection with new side tracks leading from the main track.

BALLAST

2,250 cubic yards crushed stone ballast put in between 337 and 338 mile posts.

Side Tracks

LOCATION	FOR WHOM CONSTRUCTED	FEET
Salisbury	M. L. Bean	230
Salisbury	Brown Furniture Co	175
Salisbury	Yadkin Railroad connection	2040
Rocky Ridge	Ballast track	2978
Salisbury	Standard Oil Co	240
Salisbury	Kincaid Veneering Co	315
Salisbury	C. A. Rice	420
		6398

Cross Ties

Number used in renewals, main track_____ 26,987
Number used in renewals, side tracks_____ 14,119
Number used in new side tracks _____ 6,528

                                                        _____

                                                         47,634

Switch Ties

Number of sets used in renewals _____ 64
Number of sets used in new side tracks_____ 11

                                                            _____

                                                             75

Bridges

No extensive work done.

Trestles

'No extensive work done.

Buildings

Harrisburg: New section foreman's house.

Undergrade Crossings

None.

Water Stations

Salisburg: 60,000 gallon capacity tank erected, releasing old one.

Coaling Stations

None.

Culverts

None.

Respectfully submitted,

JNO. W. THOMPSON,
Expert for North Carolina Railroad Co.

E. H. COAPMAN,
Asst. General Superintendent Southern Ry.

Greensboro, N. C., July 7, 1906.

*Mr. Samuel Spencer, President, Southern Railway Co., No. 80
Broadway, New York, and Mr. H. G. Chatham, President North
Carolina Railroad, Elkin, N. C.*

GENTLEMEN: In our report of the examination of the North
Carolina Railroad, dated Dec. 27, 1905, we gave the total number
of feet of side tracks which had been built and completed during the
year, ending Sept. 30, 1905, without specifying the length of the

tracks or the right of way of the North Carolina Railroad. We beg
to herewith submit an amended report, which will give both the
total length of tracks built and completed and the length of tracks
on the right of way of the North Carolina Railroad.

Between Goldsboro and Spencer

LOCATION	FOR WHOM CONSTRUCTED	TOTAL LENGTH	Length or Right of way
Graham	Midway Brick Co	350	350
Goldsboro	Dewey Bros	328	
Gibsonville	Minneola Manufacturing Co.	350	
Selma	N. E. Ward	600	347
Selma	Navassa Guano Co	3250	156.5
Haw River	Trollingwood Mfg. Co	2735	385
Hillsboro	Bellevue Mfg. Co	1000	585
Selma	Storage tracks	11500	11500
Durham	Bad order track	250	250
Durham	American Tobacco Co	1140	1140
Goldsboro	H. Weil & Bro	275	275
		21778	14988.5

Between Spencer and Charlotte

LOCATION	FOR WHOM CONSTRUCTED	TOTAL LENGTH	Length or Right of Way
Salisbury	M. L. Bean	230	230
Salisbury	Brown Furniture Co	175	175
Salisbury	Yadkin Railroad connection	2040	2040
Rocky Ridge	Ballast track	2978	412
Salisbury	Standard Oil Co	240	240
Salisbury	Kincaid Veneering Co	315	315
Salisbury	C. A. Rice	420	420
		6398	3832

Respectfully submitted,

JNO. W. THOMPSON,

Expert for North Carolina Railroad Co.

E. H. COAPMAN,

Asst. General Superintendent So. Ry.

Raleigh. N. C , April 4, 1906.

Mr. H. C. Chatham, President North Carolina Railroad:

SIR: Since the report of my predecessor, dated April 24. 1905, the following engine and cars have been destroyed, to-wit :

Engine No. 1724.

Box cars Nos. 3900, 3967, 6071, 6359, 7047, 7548, 8637, 8658, 10598, 10672.

Flat cars Nos. 48030, 48320, 48796, 49210.

Shanty car B-33.

The following list of equipment has replaced the above, to-wit :

Southern engine No. 1725.

Southern box cars Nos. 4042. 4922, 4975, 5040, 5189, 10168, 10249, 11002, 11462, 11662.

Flat cars Nos. 48037, 48262, 49101, 49567.

Shanty car B-25.

Hence the following is the list of equipment in possession of the Southern Railway Company belonging to the North Carolina Railroad. bearing plates or printed designation, to-wit :

Twenty-three locomotives, Nos. 1320, 1321, 1502, 1504. 1505, 1721, 1722, 1725, 1733, 1740. 1743, 1747, 1753, 1776, 1777, 1784, 1874, 1876, 1884, 1885, 1887, 1893, 1903.

Eighteen coaches, Nos. 700. 701, 702, 706, 707, 720, 721, 725, 726, 728, 729. 951, 953, 954, 1009, 1017. I231.

Four mail cars, Nos. 150, 151, 152 153.

Eight express cars, Nos. 300, 301, 302, 303, 304, 305, 312, 313.

One Superintendent's car, No. 107.

Six caboose cars, Nos. X-36, X-37, X-222, X-421, X-747, X-798.

Eight shanty cars, Nos. B-25, B-27, B 28, B-31, B-35, B-36, B-38, B-39.

One hundred and fifty-nine box cars, Nos. 1691, 3437, 3524, 3836. 3949, 3994, 4042, 4165, 4196, 4205, 4261, 4262, 4267, 4402, 4408. 4618, 4620, 4650, 4670, 4675, 4689, 4739 4790, 4841, 4847, 4851, 4868, 4881, 4919, 4922, 4975, 5029, 5040, 5067, 5089, 5141, 5172, 5189, 5217, 5291, 5319, 5397, 5439, 5503, 5512. 5580, 5621, 5622, 5623, 5624, 5625. 5626, 5628, 5629, 5630, 5631, 5633, 5634, 5637, 5640, 5641, 5642, 5723, 5803, 5899, 5906, 5933, 5963, 6016, 6045, 6095, 6098, 6102, 6108, 6132, 6151, 6157, 6195, 6307, 6334, 6368, 6404, 6420, 6440, 6458, 6490. 6493, 6513, 6527, 6581, 6597. 6618, 6632. 6684, 6788, 6805, 6868, 6871, 6883,

6898, 6901, 6939, 6970, 6973, 7011, 7119, 7144, 7239, 7281, 7327, 7
7385, 7457, 7495, 7539, 7540, 7612, 7660, 8208, 8209, 8212, 8218, 8
8610, 8651, 8734, 9402, 9458, 9513, 9515, 9523, 9542, 9651, 9674, 9
9793, 9802, 10075, 10095, 10126, 10168, 10249, 10311, 10634, 10
10821, 11002, 11031, 11073, 11221, 11287, 11462, 11471, 11562, 11
22208, 22365, 22371, 22406.

Seventy-four flat cars. Nos. 46970, 46971, 48023, 48037, 48
48045, 48047, 48056, 48064, 48081, 48089, 48108, 48140, 48165, 48
48180, 48189, 48197, 48208, 48215, 48223, 48262, 48270, 48271, 48
48316, 48429, 48486, 48487, 48491, 48492, 48496, 48497, 48499, 48
48504, 48505, 48506, 48507, 48527, 48540, 48548, 48553, 48562, 48
48648, 48687, 48690, 48694, 48699, 48711, 48734, 48770, 48791, 48
48879, 48890, 48920, 48946, 49008, 49016, 49026, 49030, 49101, 49
49193, 49259, 49567, 49639, 49640, 49723, 49793, 49795, 50071.

Very respectfully,

JNO. W. THOMPSON,
Expert for North Carolina Railroa

CPSIA information can be obtained
at www.ICGtesting.com
Printed in the USA
LVHW051500051118
596010LV00013B/1262/P